anythink

D0478708

B Is for Bee

ABCs of Endangered Insects

by Catherine Ipcizade

CAPSTONE PRESS

a capstone imprint

A+ Books are published by Capstone Press,
1710 Roe Crest Drive, North Mankato, Minnesota 56003
www.mycapstone.com

Library of Congress Cataloging-in-Publication Data
Library of Congress Cataloging-in-Publication data is available on the Library of Congress website.
ISBN 978-1-4914-8035-9 (library binding)
ISBN 978-1-4914-8406-7 (eBook PDF)
Summary: Describes endangered insects of the world by assigning
a species or insect-related term to each letter of the alphabet.

Editorial Credits:
Jill Kalz, editor; Bobbie Nuytten, designer; Jo Miller, media researcher;
Katy LaVigne, production specialist

Special thanks to Erin Hodgson, Associate Professor and Extension Entomologist,
Iowa State University; and Michael Francis for their expertise.

Image Credits:
Alamy: blickwinkel, cover (bottom right), 10, 23, DEEPU SG, 26, Purestock, 25; Getty Images: National Geographic/Joel Sartone, 22; Glow Images: Deposit Photos, 27, Minden Pictures: FLPA/ Larry West, 14, Simon Colmer, 1 (right), 9; National Geographic Creative: Joel Sartore, cover (bottom left), 7, 12; Newscom: Minden Pictures/Mark Moffett, 4, Photoshot/NHPA/Thomas Kitchin & Victoria Hurst, 15; Science Source, cover (bottom middle), 24; Shutterstock: Air Images, 28, Aleksey Stemmer, 6, Amy Johansson, 11, Apinan, cover (top), David Byron Keener, 1 (left), 16, Fred Young, 19, Irina Kozorog, 20, LilKar, 21, Lusine, 5, Paul Sparks, 8, Trofimov Denis, 29; Wikimedia: Franco Folini from San Francisco, USA, 17, U.S. Fish & Wildlife Service - Pacific Region, 18, U.S. Fish and Wildlife Service, Pacific Southwest Region, 13

Design Elements:
Shutterstock: Potapov Alexander, Ramona Heim

Printed and bound in the USA.
009690F16

Note to Parents, Teachers, and Librarians

The E for Endangered series supports national science standards related to zoology. This book describes and illustrates insects. The images support early readers in understanding the text. The repetition of words and phrases helps early readers learn new words. This book also introduces early readers to subject-specific vocabulary words, which are defined in the Glossary section. Early readers may need assistance to read some words and to use the Share the Facts, Glossary, Internet Sites, Critical Thinking Using the Common Core, Read More, and Index sections of the book.

ENDANGERED!

What does it mean to be endangered?

Endangered plants and animals are at high risk of disappearing. Our planet may lose them forever because of habitat loss, hunting, or other threats. When one species goes away, the loss often hurts other species. All life on Earth is connected in some way.

All of the insects in this book are in trouble. They are either near threatened (at some risk), vulnerable (at more risk), or endangered. Their numbers are small. But they don't have to disappear. You can help by reading more about them and sharing what you learn with others.

Aa:
arthropod

Arthropods make up the world's largest group of animals. They all share certain features. They have segmented bodies, lots of legs, and exoskeletons. All insects are arthropods. So are animals such as spiders, lobsters, centipedes, and shrimp.

AMERICAN BURYING BEETLE

Bb:

bee

Bees are covered with stiff hairs. When a bee lands on a flower, small grains called pollen stick to the hairs. Pollen is carried to other flowers as the bee visits them. Some plants need pollination to make seeds or fruit. Without bees, many plants would die out. Habitat loss is affecting honeybees, yellowbanded bumblebees, and many other bee species.

HONEYBEE

Cc: cockroach

Madagascar hissing cockroaches aren't endangered, but their habitat is! These large, loud insects live only in Madagascar, an island off the coast of Africa. They nest in forests, under wet leaves or fallen logs. About 80 percent of the island's forests have been destroyed. The trees are cut down for lumber or to make room for farms.

Dd:
Delhi Sands flower-loving fly

Delhi Sands flower-loving flies are native to California. Their name comes from the type of sand in which female flies lay their eggs. The hummingbird-like flies have a long feeding tube called a proboscis. They use it to suck up flower nectar. The flies can also fly in place while feeding on flowers—just like hummingbirds!

Ee:
emerald dragonfly

Hine's emerald dragonflies have bright, green eyes and shiny, green bodies. They live in marshes and meadows in only a few northern U.S. states. The dragonflies take two to four years to become adults. During this growing period, many become food for fish. As adults the dragonflies live only four to five weeks.

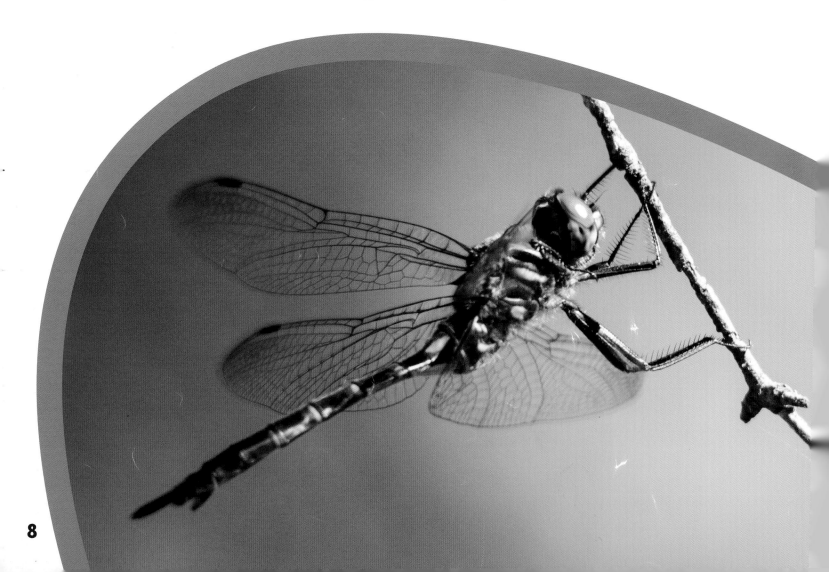

Ff:
Fregate Island

Fregate Island giant tenebrionid (TEH-neh-bree-eh-ned) beetles are large, flightless insects. They live only in forests on Fregate Island, in the western Indian Ocean. The beetles hide during the day and feed at night. When in danger, they release a smelly, purple liquid.

Gg: grasshopper

European giant steppe grasshoppers live in dry, flat, treeless areas. They are found mostly in southern France, Italy, Slovenia, Bosnia and Herzegovina, and Croatia. Habitat loss is the greatest danger for these flightless grasshoppers. Their habitat also makes for good building and animal grazing sites.

Hh:
habitat loss

Habitat loss is a big reason why insects become endangered. When people clear land to farm or to build roads and cities, insects can no longer live in those places. Insects cannot always move to new places. The new places may not have what the insects need. The insects may be forced to compete for food or space with animals already living there.

Ii:
interfere

To interfere is to disturb or barge into. When people clear land or dirty the air and water, they interfere with plant and animal habitats. As a result, species may become endangered. As the city of San Francisco, California, grew, it shrunk the Xerces blue butterflies' habitat. The insects started to die off. They became one of the first extinct butterflies in North America.

Jj:
June beetle

Casey's June beetles measure 1 to 2 inches (2.5–5 centimeters) long and are found only in southern California. They live in underground burrows most of the year. In spring the beetles crawl out to find mates. Males can fly, but females cannot.

Kk: Karner blue butterfly

Karner blue butterflies are small in number and small in size. Their wingspan measures only about 1 inch (2.5 cm). Males are silvery blue on top. Females are grayish brown. Both males and females have orange and black markings on the undersides of the wings. Karner blues live in the northern United States, in grassland areas from Wisconsin to New Hampshire.

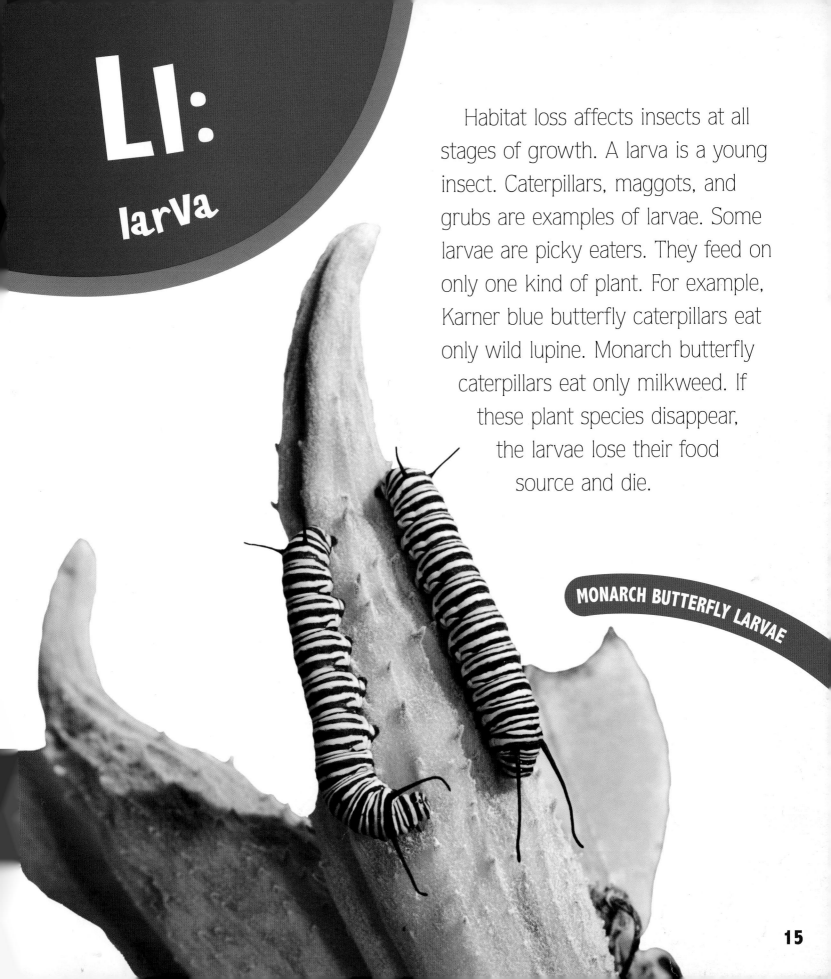

Ll:
larva

Habitat loss affects insects at all stages of growth. A larva is a young insect. Caterpillars, maggots, and grubs are examples of larvae. Some larvae are picky eaters. They feed on only one kind of plant. For example, Karner blue butterfly caterpillars eat only wild lupine. Monarch butterfly caterpillars eat only milkweed. If these plant species disappear, the larvae lose their food source and die.

MONARCH BUTTERFLY LARVAE

Mm: monarch butterfly

Monarch butterflies need milkweed to live. They lay their eggs on the underside of the leaves. Once the larvae hatch, they feed on the milkweed. The milky sap in milkweed is poisonous, but it doesn't hurt these caterpillars. However, if other animals eat them, they will get sick. Predators quickly learn to stay away from these colorful insects.

Nn:
Navajo Jerusalem cricket

Navajo Jerusalem crickets live in the southwestern United States and parts of Mexico. Unlike other species, Navajo Jerusalem crickets don't chirp. They hiss. They hide during the day and feed at night. Nearly 2 inches (5 cm) long, these large crickets are mostly harmless, but they can bite.

Oo:
Oceanic Hawaiian damselfly

Oceanic Hawaiian damselflies are fierce predators. They swoop quickly through the air to grab their prey. But when they are the ones being hunted, they act much differently. When they think they may be caught, Oceanic Hawaiian damselflies pretend to be dead.

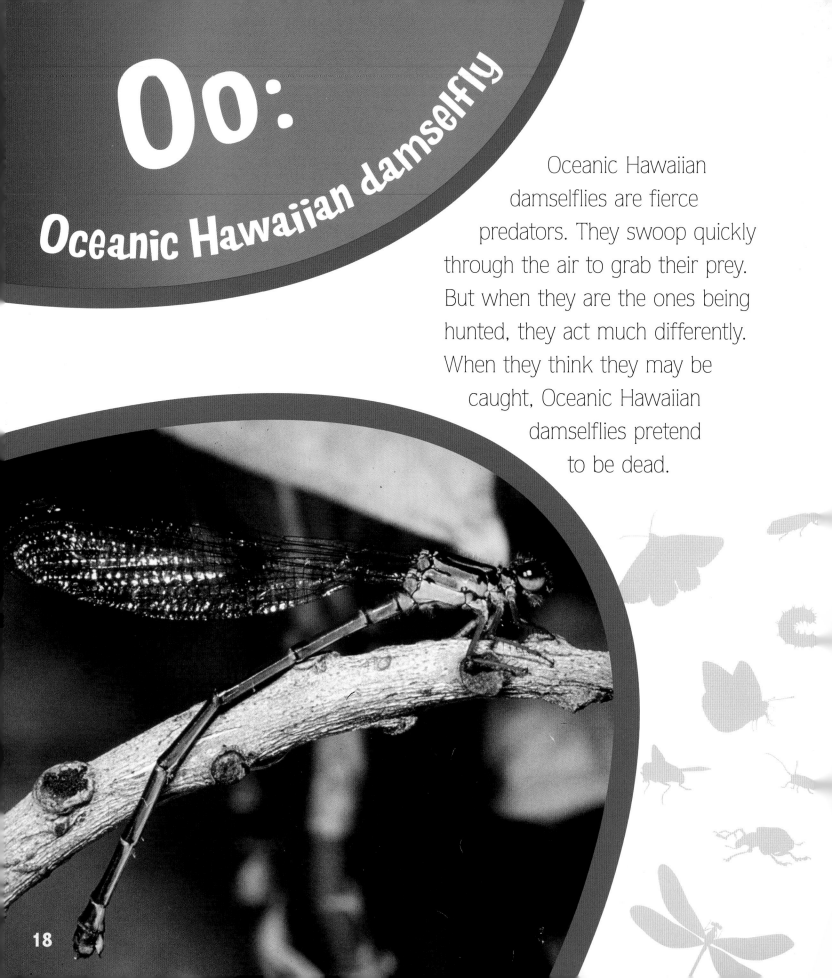

Pp:
pesticide

Pesticides are chemicals. They're used to prevent, control, or kill unwanted plants and animals. People commonly use pesticides on weeds, mice, and insects. Sometimes pesticides affect more than the unwanted species. They change the habitats and food sources for many other plants and animals. The changes can put those species in danger of disappearing.

Qq: quintillion

There are about 10 quintillion insects alive today. That means there are about 170 insects in the world for every person on Earth. So far, scientists have named about 1 million insect species. It is thought there could be as many as 9 million more to be discovered!

Rr:
resource

Although some insects are considered pests, many provide resources we need. Bees make honey and pollinate plants. Moths are pollinators too. Silkworm caterpillars give us silk. Other insects are important food sources in many food chains.

Ss:
Salt Creek tiger beetle

Salt Creek tiger beetles are one of the rarest insects in the world. They make their homes in a small part of Nebraska, in moist, muddy areas. The beetles measure just a half-inch (1 cm) long. They get their name from the way the adults use their mouthparts to grab prey—like tigers use their teeth.

Tt:
Tansy beetle

Tansy beetles are bright green insects with a copper glow. As adults they measure less than a half-inch (1 cm) long. They get their name from a plant they eat. Tansy has yellow button-like flowers and grows in wetlands and along riverbanks. Tansy beetles live in Europe, from Sweden to Italy.

Uu:
U.S. Fish and Wildlife Service

The U.S. Fish and Wildlife Service (FWS) protects plants and animals. One insect species it's trying to save is the mission blue butterfly. These endangered butterflies live only in California, in places where lupine plants grow. As areas of lupines disappear, so do the butterflies. The FWS is helping mission blues by removing plants and pests that harm lupines. Removal is often done with controlled fires.

Vv:
Palos Verde blue butterfly

Palos Verde blue butterflies live only in a small coastal area south of Los Angeles, California. For a long time, people thought they were extinct. But in 1994 a group of about 60 Palos Verde blue butterflies were rediscovered. These tiny insects lay their eggs in locoweed or deerweed flowers. Lack of good rainfall in recent years has hurt the plants and butterflies.

Ww:

wing

Wings help many insects travel to find food, mates, and homes. They help them escape from danger. Sometimes insect wings are so beautiful that people want to keep them in collections. Queen Alexandra's birdwings are the largest known butterflies. Their wings measure 11 inches (28 cm) from wingtip to wingtip.

Xx:
eXtinct

When a species becomes extinct, it is no longer found on Earth. We lose it forever. Losing even one kind of plant or animal affects our world. It creates a chain reaction that touches countless other species. Insects play a huge role in our lives. They are predators, recyclers, silk makers, composters, and food makers.

Yy:
you

You can protect insects in small ways and make a big difference. Grow a mix of plants that bloom from spring to fall. The flowers will provide insects with lots of pollen and nectar to feed on. Don't use bug zappers. Wait awhile before raking and bagging fall leaves. Some insects count on those leaves for food.

Zz: buzz

The sound of buzzing bees is a good sign. It tells us that plants are being pollinated. Bumblebees and honeybees flap their wings about 230 times per second. The flapping makes the bees' *buzz* sound. Butterflies, by contrast, flap their wings only 5 to 20 times per second—not fast enough for us to hear a buzz.

SHARE THE FACTS

- In some parts of the world, people eat insects, such as crickets and grasshoppers. They may fry, bake, or roast them. They may even dip them in chocolate.

- Ninety percent of the vitamin C people need to stay healthy comes from insect-pollinated plants.

- One southeastern blueberry bee pollinates enough plants in its lifetime to help make 6,000 tasty blueberries.

- American burying beetles get their name from what they do: bury dead animals. A female beetle lays her eggs near a buried animal, which will be food for her young when they hatch.

- Bees aren't the only pollinators in the world. Butterflies, moths, bats, and birds are also major pollinators.

- Hine's emerald dragonflies are one of many species on the U.S. List of Endangered and Threatened Wildlife and Plants. It is against the law to harm, collect, or kill them without special permission.

- American burying beetles are about 1.5 inches (3.8 cm) long. They aren't very big, but they are hardy fliers. They can travel more than a half-mile (1 kilometer) in one night.

- Queen Alexandra's birdwings are poisonous. Animals get very sick if they eat them. The butterflies' bright colors warn hungry animals to stay away.

GLOSSARY

endangered—at risk of disappearing forever

exoskeleton—the hard outer layer of an insect; the exoskeleton protects the insect from predators and from drying out

extinct—when a species no longer exists on Earth

habitat—a place where an animal can find its food, water, shelter, and space to live

larva—a young insect or other animal without a backbone; grubs are the larvae of beetles

near threatened—could become endangered in the near future

nectar—a sweet liquid found in many flowers

pesticide—a chemical that controls unwanted plants and animals

pollinate—to carry pollen from flower to flower; pollination helps plants make seeds

predator—an animal that hunts and eats other animals

protect—to save from danger

segmented—made of many parts

species—a group of plants or animals that share common traits

vulnerable—at high risk of becoming endangered

INTERNET SITES

FactHound offers a safe, fun way to find Internet sites related to this book. All of the sites on FactHound have been researched by our staff.

Here's all you do:

Visit *www.facthound.com*

Type in this code: 9781491480359

 Check out projects, games and lots more at **www.capstonekids.com**

CRITICAL THINKING
USING THE COMMON CORE

1. Name three features that all arthropods share. (Key Ideas and Details)

2. Why are bees important? (Key Ideas and Details)

3. "When one species goes away, the loss often hurts other species." Show the connection between plants and insects by using monarch butterflies or Karner blue butterflies as an example. (Integration of Knowledge and Ideas)

READ MORE

Bell, Samantha. *12 Insects Back from the Brink.* Back from the Brink. North Mankato, Minn.: 12-Story Library, 2015.

Boothroyd, Jennifer. *Endangered and Extinct Invertebrates.* Animals in Danger. Minneapolis: Lerner Publications Company, 2014.

Gagne, Tammy. *The Most Endangered Animals in the World.* All About Animals. North Mankato, Minn.: Capstone Press, 2015.

INDEX